MATISSE: 50 YEARS OF HIS GRAPHIC ART

2

MATISSE

50 YEARS OF HIS GRAPHIC ART

TEXT BY WILLIAM S. LIEBERMAN

NEW YORK

GEORGE BRAZILLER, INC.

CONTENTS

This book gathers together a selection of Henri Matisse's graphic work produced during a half century. It does not include drawings nor does it attempt a *catalogue raisonné* of his prints.[1] The survey, however, offers a comprehensive review of his work in the many print media he chose to use—drypoint, etching, lithography, linoleum cut, monotype and aquatint. It also reproduces pages from those books Matisse illustrated with original prints. His illustrations for *Jazz,* a brilliant creation of his last years, were conceived to be executed by craftsmen. They are not in any strict sense "originals" but since Matisse directed their entire production they are included here.

nlike Picasso, Matisse never sustained a continuous level of interest in printmaking. His accomplishment as an etcher and lithographer was prodigious, but it was concentrated into relatively short periods throughout his career. In 1914, for instance, he turned to printmaking with such enthusiasm that surely he sought refreshment from easel painting in the techniques of minor media.

Matisse first worked on copper in 1903. His early prints are tentative essays, the most assured of which, the *Self Portrait as an Etcher,* offers a factual reflection of the artist's image at the age of thirty-three. The other plates are frankly exercises, drypoint studies of a woman in street costume, a half dozen sketches of the nude. Matisse's casual approach is exemplified by one etching in which heads of the artist's son and daughter accompany a pair of views of the same nude.

In 1906 Matisse composed his first lithographs and linoleum cuts.[2] The lithographs number twelve, the linoleum cuts three.[3] With one exception—a sketch of the harbor at Collioure, which he presented to Gertrude Stein—the subjects are either heads of women, or full figures drawn standing, seated or crouching. There is little in these nudes to titillate the erotic sensibility of the spectator. The poses are somewhat unflattering, even distorted, and the series has often been described as *fauve.* Actually the prints are more reminiscent of Matisse's sculpture than of his painting.

After a lapse of several years Matisse returned to printmaking in three media: within a few months in 1914 he produced nine or ten lithographs, at least fourteen monotypes and some fifty etchings. As nudes the lithographs seem somewhat more seductive than the earlier series of 1906. The designs are free, large,[4] and the attitudes more elegant. The placement of the figure in relation to the printed sheet is arresting: details of the torso are isolated and swept into the rhythm of Matisse's line.

The monotypes of 1914 offer a greater variety of subjects: nudes and, in addition, portraits, still lives and interior scenes. Meticulously printed, probably from copper plates, each is of course unique. Matisse is reported to have been "very much pleased with those prints of his of white lines on a black background."[5] One may be a self portrait, and all but one are reproduced here. Matisse made no monotypes after 1914.

The etchings of the same year are much more intimate than the lithographs or monotypes. Mostly portraits of friends and family, they build a brilliant sequence of quick and informal characterizations: the wives of the painters Galanis and Gris,[6] Mme Vignier and her daughter Irène, Yvonne Landsberg,[7] the artist's wife and children, and—surprising to a student of Matisse's art—several men, among

Nude. 1904? Lithograph (29), 11¾₁₆ x 9¹⁵⁄₁₆ inches (284 x 253 mm). The Museum of Modern Art, New York, Mrs. John D. Rockefeller, Jr. Purchase Fund

them the Spaniards Massia, Iturrino and Olivares, the British museologist Matthew Stewart Prichard and the American painter Walter Pach.

The portraits were finished with astonishing speed after careful consideration of the sitter. The drawing is quick and decisive. Like all of Matisse's etchings, each is distinguished by its simplicity. Individual features are reduced to vivid details, and often the contours of the face fill the rectangular frame of the copper plate. The figure is treated at greater length only occasionally. Several friends sat more than once, and in the series there are as many as seven different likenesses of the same individual. Only one professional model seems to have posed, "Loulou," who appears head, front and back.

To the gallery of miniature portraits Matisse added a few studies of the nude and a sketch of foliage.[8] He had originally intended to gather the portraits as an album; but instead the etchings were issued separately in editions of five to fifteen proofs each.

Walter Pach has written a lively account of Matisse as a print portraitist in 1914.[9] One October morning in Paris the two had been "talking art" for several hours. Pach looked at the time and said:

"I didn't know it was so late. I have an appointment and must be off in less than ten minutes."

"I'd like to do an etching of you."

"Fine. When shall I come?"

"I'll do it right now. I have a plate ready."

"But I've got to meet M. Hessel for lunch. I've got to leave in five minutes . . ."

"All right. I'll do it in five minutes."

Matisse placed his watch on the table, set to work and within five minutes outlined the drawing on the plate.

"This isn't serious. I got interested in what you were saying about Rembrandt, and I wanted to set down an impression of you then and there. But come on Sunday morning and we'll have time for a real one."

When Pach returned, he found the etching already printed. There were a few tiny, unimportant spots from "foul" biting of the etching acid. Matisse said, "I did not do those. God did. What God does is well done; it is only what men do . . ."

Pach sat again and for three hours Matisse sketched other plates. But, the American remembers, "we looked at the little five-minute etching . . . it had just the life that the more heavily worked things had lost."

Matisse's first prints, cumulatively significant as a graphic production, were the lithographs, monotypes and etchings of 1914. During the next decade Matisse etched a few plates but not until 1922 does he seem to have resumed working on stone. He began with some hesitation, but in 1925 alone he printed more than twenty lithographs. The most notable is a progression of seated figures which reaches a climax in two large versions of a nude in an armchair and culminates in the voluptuous *Odalisque in Striped Pantaloons*.

Between 1926 and 1930 Matisse increased his yearly manufacture of lithographs. The subjects of some sixty prints are paid models nude or draped. They appear singly, frequently surrounded by accessories of flowers, fabrics or furniture. Matisse's drawing varies from spontaneous studies in line to strongly modeled, meticulous delineations. Sometimes the pose is conventional, sometimes radically contorted. Occasionally the model is seen from above and the arabesques formed by the accessories and figure merge into one fluid pattern.

In his definitive *Matisse: His Art and His Public*, Alfred H. Barr, Jr., concisely summarizes the production of 1926–30. The lithographs "reflect to some degree the reaction toward the bolder, more experimental spirit which generally marks the painting and sculpture of that period. The brilliant outline portrait of the pianist Alfred Cortot is the most striking print of 1926–27 but the very large, fluently drawn and delicately modeled *Reclining Odalisque* is more characteristic.

"Most of the lithographs published in 1927 are devoted to a new subject for Matisse—the ballet dancer—inspired perhaps by his renewed contact with Diaghilev . . . .[10] In this series, most of which was issued in the portfolio *Dix Danseuses*,[11] the ballerina is conventionally costumed . . . . Matisse draws her standing, seated or reclining but, curiously, never dancing or practicing at the bar. . . .

"Possibly Matisse published no stones in 1928 but the twenty or so lithographs of 1929 cover subjects which appear in his painting of 1928. . . . More than half the lithographs . . . are studies of the model seen from various angles as she reclines on a couch surrounded by patterned textiles, flowers, the familiar brass stove, and the Louis XV table. . . .

"The most remarkable lithographs . . . are without question the vivid, sharply modeled compositions in which details . . . are more elaborately rendered than in any other mature works of Matisse. In the *Odalisque in a Tulle Skirt*, the transparent texture of the garment, the inlay of the Moorish chair and tabouret are precisely simulated not only in the detail but in color values. . . . *The White Boa*, a portrait study of the same model, is equally remarkable for its almost photographic effect of light, color and texture but, on close inspection, one finds that the detail has been suggested with extraordinary economy."[12]

Suddenly, at the end of the decade, Matisse resumed etching. Within a few months he produced a constellation of about one hundred and twenty-five plates, studies of nudes and odalisques, and a series of girls gazing at goldfish. Again, as in 1914, Matisse worked directly on the plate from the model. Sometimes, like the lithographs, the etchings repeat or anticipate motifs in his painting. Usually, although often similar in subject, they remain distinct.

At first this series of etchings may seem incidental but, freshly examined, it reduces daring syncopations of a pose or movement into an essential of lines. Matisse plays endless variations on the same themes. The concise reductions of the etchings of 1929 dispel the still and heavy atmosphere of the seraglio which permeates the lithographs of the late 20s. Matisse's line is lively and inquisitive as it dances out the tensions and balances which sustain the series.

After 1930 Matisse's principal energies as a printmaker were devoted to the illustration of books.

In any discussion of modern French painters as illustrators, it must seem surprising that Matisse and Ambroise Vollard never joined in collaboration. In 1900, with the publication of Bonnard's lithographs to Verlaine's *Parallèlement*, Vollard had established the archetype of books illustrated by artists of the School of Paris. During the next four decades he remained their foremost publisher.[13]

Although Vollard will be remembered as an editor of fine books and prints, his livelihood depended upon his activities as a picture dealer. Among the first to show and sell the paintings of Cézanne and Picasso, he also sponsored Matisse's first one-man exhibition.[14] Their association was brief. A collaboration might have produced a magnificent book, but perhaps Matisse found Vollard too difficult and

Reclining Odalisque. 1926.
Lithograph (81), 17⅛ x
31¼ inches (435 x 794
mm). The Museum of
Modern Art, New York,
gift of Mrs. Saidie A. May

11

dilatory an impresario. His only contribution to the publisher's ventures was a single etching delivered for a proposed portfolio of nudes.[15]

At the age of sixty-three when Matisse completed his first illustrated book, most of his younger contemporaries had filled many such commissions.[16] Indeed, in the library of illustrations by artists of the School of Paris, only a volume by Matisse was lacking.[17]

It was a young and courageous Swiss publisher who launched Matisse in his tardy debut in 1932. The previous year Albert Skira had presented Picasso's etched illustrations to Ovid's *Metamorphoses*. Skira's second volume was to be equally distinguished. He asked Picasso's stellar rival to illustrate the poems of Mallarmé. Matisse responded with enthusiasm.

"This is the work I have completed after reading Mallarmé with pleasure. . . . The drawing is not massed toward the center as usual but spreads across the entire page. The problem was to balance each pair of facing pages—the one with the etching white, the other with the typography relatively black. I achieved this by modifying my arabesques in such a way that the spectator's attention would be interested as much by the entire page as by the promise of reading the text."[18]

The subject matter of the twenty-nine illustrations, like that of the poems themselves, varies considerably. The flowing alternations of Matisse's draughtsmanship, however, lend a continuity and create a deceptive effect of effortless spontaneity. Matisse chose the point of a sapphire for his etching needle which, by its very precision, imposes a quick irrevocable line. Some designs make casual reference to his Tahitian voyage of 1930; others recall earlier figure compositions. Never literal, each illustration evokes in a vivid graphic image a specific title or phrase. Longer poems, such as "L'Après-midi d'un faune" and "Hérodiade," are treated at greater length. The most memorable illustration, one of unaccustomed psychological intensity, is the portrait which accompanies the sonnet "Tombeau de Baudelaire."[19]

A second commission for book illustration was arranged by long-distance telephone.[20] For $5000 Matisse agreed to supply six etchings for an edition of James Joyce's *Ulysses*. The volume was designed by the late George Macy and published for his Limited Editions Club in New York in 1935. In comparison with the Mallarmé, Matisse's contribution was slight and, as illustration, unsuccessful. He was perhaps aware of the parallel construction between *Ulysses* and the *Odyssey*.[21] At any rate he chose to illustrate Homer rather than Joyce.

Five encounters of Ulysses are represented: Calypso, Aeolus, Polyphemus, Nausicaä, Circe and, for the homecoming, a view of Ithaca. The designs were drawn through paper onto a soft ground which covered the copper plates to be etched. This allowed Matisse to delineate as well as to shade as if with crayon or

12

charcoal. In the book, each etching is accompanied by two to five preparatory sketches. The preliminary drawings come to life in a way the finished prints do not. For sheer readability, the double columns of the Limited Editions text may be the most satisfactory presentation of *Ulysses*. But as the illustrator Matisse did justice neither to Joyce nor to himself.[22]

During the 30s Matisse continued to print a few etchings and lithographs each year, but his activity as a printmaker never exceeded the prolific production of 1914 or the late 20s. By 1935 he had made some two hundred intaglio plates, three linoleum cuts, almost a hundred and fifty lithographs as well as the early suite of monotypes. He had also completed commissions for two illustrated books. Printmaking had allowed him to distill or elaborate in other media themes on which he had been working as a painter. With fresh inspiration, particularly in illustration, printmaking had expanded the iconography of his art as well.

After 1941 a series of major operations left Matisse an invalid, and he devoted a major part of his time to book illustration. Martin Fabiani, a former associate of Vollard,[23] managed to become a successful dealer during the German occupation of France and, in 1944, published Matisse's third illustrated book.[24] The text consists of extracts from Henry de Montherlant's *Les Crétois*.

The painter and the writer had met in Nice in the winter of 1937. Montherlant sat for his portrait and Matisse considered illustrating his *La Rose de Sable*. "It became necessary to abandon this project. Each time an image began to form in my mind, the end of the story would stop me. Montherlant's description was thorough and complete. I could add nothing." Soon after, however, Matisse did undertake to interpret two selections from *Les Crétois:* "Pasiphaé," a play in verse,[25] and "Chant de Minos," a poem.

For the *Pasiphaé-Chant de Minos,* Matisse returned to one of his favorite graphic media, linoleum cut. These blocks, however, differ radically from those of 1906. Instead of carving away to leave a design in relief which prints as black, Matisse retained most of the linoleum's surface. The solid black rectangle of the uncut surface serves as a background to the engraved composition it contains. When inked the incised line of the design prints as white.

Somewhat fussily Matisse cautions: "The lino should not be used as a cheap substitute for wood because it gives to a print its own special character, quite different from woodcut, and therefore should be studied. The gouge is controlled directly by the sensibility of the engraver. Indeed this is so true that the least distraction during the execution of a line causes a slight pressure of the fingers on the

gouge and influences the drawing for the worse. Engraving on the linoleum is a true medium for the painter illustrator."

Once again Matisse expands suggestions from a poet's verse into his own personal imagery. The result is more studied than the Mallarmé and Matisse took great care in the composition of the book as a whole. "A single white line on an absolutely black background. . . . The problem is the same as for the Mallarmé, but the two elements are reversed. How to balance the black page without text with the comparatively white page of typography? . . . by bringing together the page engraved and the page of type . . . a wide margin surrounding both pages completely masses them together. . . . I had a definite feeling of a somewhat sinister character of a book in black and white. However, a book generally seems like that. But in this case the large page almost entirely black seemed a bit funereal. Then I thought of red initials. . . . Starting out with capitals that were picturesque, fantastic, the inventions of a painter, I was obliged to change to a more severe and classic conception of lettering in keeping with the elements of typography and engraving already chosen. . . . So then: Black, White, Red—not so bad."

Matisse's enthusiasm for linoleum cut was not satisfied by the illustrations to Montherlant alone. He incised about two dozen other prints—heads of women and

Rejected plate illustrating *L'Après-midi d'un faune*, page 81 of *Poésies de Stéphane Mallarmé*, 1932. 11¾ x 9⅞ inches (298 x 240 mm). The Baltimore Museum of Art, Cone Collection

still lives of fruit. Again, in 1952, he would produce another series of independent prints, but between 1941 and 1950 his principal activity as a printmaker continued to be illustration. Often he was at work on several projects at the same time and their order of publication does not necessarily follow their sequence of composition.

A certain pedestrian sameness characterizes Matisse's next four volumes—*Visages, Repli,* a *Lettres Portugaises* and a *Fleurs du Mal,* all begun in 1943 and 1944 and issued during the winter of 1946–47. The author of *Visages,* Pierre Reverdy, was a friend of Matisse. So was André Rouveyre, the caricaturist and author of *Repli,* who lived at Vence where Matisse had moved in 1943.[26] Both books contain some dozen lithographs of heads as well as ornaments cut in linoleum.

For Efstratios Tériade,[27] like Skira a leading publisher of fine editions, Matisse adorned the five letters of the Portuguese nun, a dependable inspiration for artists good and bad. Matisse supervised the entire layout. The lithographs, charming if repetitive, offer a profusion of initials and leaves printed in violet, and a sequence of portraits of the cowled epistolarian herself.

A Baudelaire by Matisse should have been an important publishing event. It was not. The artist conceived a *Fleurs du Mal* with more than thirty lithographs and

15

twice as many wood engravings. Dry weather unfortunately ruined the transfer paper on which Matisse had drawn. Finally the illustrations, mostly female heads, were photographed and mechanically reproduced. They bear little affinity to the passion of the poems. A portrait of Baudelaire reaffirms that Matisse's tribute to the poet had been the earlier, stark and abbreviated mask for Mallarmé's sonnet.

During the composition of *Visages, Repli, Lettres Portugaises* and *Fleurs du Mal,* Matisse was devoting his best energies to three other books. The first, *Jazz,* was published by Tériade. The illustrations are not original prints but splendid color reproductions of designs Matisse worked out with scissors, paste and pins.[28] He composed *Jazz* during a twelve months' confinement to his bed in 1944. When the book was issued in 1947, he appeared not only as illustrator but as author as well.

In the fall of 1941 Skira had visited Matisse in Nice. The painter spoke of a project he had often considered, an illustrated anthology of Ronsard's love poems. The book was planned to contain some thirty lithographs to be printed in Switzerland. The first printing of the text did not suit Matisse's illustrations, so a new type face was selected, a font of rather worn Caslon. A second proof of the text was pulled for Matisse's use in making the illustrations. The war delayed another meeting until 1946. The artist had so expanded the original plan that when the Caslon was shipped from Geneva to Paris it had to be reset for a third time. After eight months the text pages were ready for the printing of the illustrations. But again misfortune struck. The sheets had turned yellow, the edition had to be scrapped, the Caslon type was too worn to be used again. After a long search Skira found William Caslon's original molds and a new font was cast. Matisse meanwhile had changed the color of the ink and had quadrupled the number of illustrations. The fourth and final printing was not made until the spring of 1948—seven years after the project had been initiated.

The love lavished upon the Ronsard is apparent as one turns its pages. The format is large and handsome. To his own choice of poems Matisse drew one hundred and twenty-six lithographs printed in brown on an off-white paper. In the Ronsard, unlike the Mallarmé or the Montherlant, Matisse does not stress a left-hand right-hand balance between text and illustration. The two are composed together. A scene of a woman bathing under a willow covers an entire folio; a pattern of leaves lightly embroiders a double spread of text pages; female heads, fragments of a nude, flowers, fruit, decorate other pages of poems; larger full-page illustrations suggest in a few sure lines scenes of pastoral romance, the reverberations of a kiss, the silhouette of a vase, the song of birds. The conception of each page is fresh and unexpected, as lyric and graceful as the poems themselves.

After this tribute to Ronsard, Matisse made an elaborate bow to another poet, Charles d'Orléans. In a large notebook of a hundred pages Matisse penned forty poems and ornamented the manuscript with color crayons. As an introduction, the first four pages are covered with fleurs-de-lis, the royal emblem of France chosen by Charles' grandfather. A gay title page in blue and red faces a noble profile portrait of the author. The fleurs-de-lis motive is thereafter repeated on each left-hand page. The lilies of France vary in size, number and arrangement. The leaves themselves are drawn in two colors, the combination changing with each page. Opposite these fields appear the various rondels, ballads and songs. On the right-hand pages Matisse copied the courtly verses in pen and ink and framed each poem with a witty rococo border. Five times the pages are interrupted by illustrations—three portraits of women, a meadow of rabbits and a nude enshrined in a flower.

It is impossible not to share Matisse's lighthearted pleasure in the creation of this book. He delights in teasing his ingenuity as far as possible within the arbitrary limits of the fleurs-de-lis foliates. The brightly colored illuminations are elegant, playful and extravagant.[29]

The *Poèmes de Charles d'Orléans* is the last of eight illustrated books Matisse completed during the decade of the 40s. During the winter of 1951–52 he returned to print-making as such and drew an important series of about twenty aquatints.[30] These consist mostly of women's heads freely brushed onto the plate to create, when printed, the effect of bold drawings in ink. He also signed a few lithographed sheets which could be sold for the profit of the Dominican Nuns of Vence whose chapel he had constructed and decorated.

Book illustration was an endeavor admirably suited to Matisse's last years. During his increasingly prolonged confinements in bed at Nice, Vence, Paris and then Nice again, he could easily spread before him the materials and texts for his projects. Illustration demanded less physical exertion than painting, and peace of mind and contentment characterize the presentation of *Jazz,* the Ronsard and the Charles d'Orléans.

When supported by an enthusiastic publisher such as Skira or Tériade—expense and time cannot be considered—Matisse had no rival as an illustrator.[31] He responded most readily to his favorite authors and believed that "the artist to make the most of his gifts must be careful not to adhere too slavishly to the text. On the contrary he must work freely, his own sensibility enriched through contact with the poet he is to illustrate.

"I do not distinguish between the construction of a book and that of a painting, and I always work from the simple to the complex, yet always ready at any moment to reconceive in simplicity. . . . Put your work back on the anvil twenty times and begin over again until you are satisfied."

The past six decades have witnessed a development in printmaking so extraordinary that today fine prints have assumed an unprecedented importance. Never before have so many of the foremost painters of any period devoted so much of their best energies to the production of original prints.

Recently there has been a revived enthusiasm for work in color, while in size prints themselves have outgrown the confines of the collector's portfolio. This increasing emphasis on color and scale has been encouraged by the public—today most prints are produced and purchased not for study but for prominent display on the walls of homes and museums.

Matisse, however, remained faithful to the custom of black and white, nor is the size of any of his single prints excessive. Only in illustration, in his last years, did he essay color and it must be remembered that the sheets for *Jazz* are no more than meticulous reproductions of his original collage designs.

Picasso, Rouault and Villon sustained a continuous interest in printmaking throughout their careers. Matisse did not, and perhaps his graphic *oeuvre* is less varied and less important in relation to his painting. But his accomplishment in black and white, limited though it may be to specific moments during a half century, is a brilliant example of the tradition of *peintre graveur*.

WILLIAM S. LIEBERMAN

1. For several years Matisse's daughter, Mme Georges Duthuit, has been preparing a definitive catalog of her father's prints. Mr. Carl O. Schniewind, Curator of Prints and Drawings at the Art Institute of Chicago, has also established a working catalog of Matisse's graphic *oeuvre.* Details as to paper and *tirage* should properly await the publication of their compilations. Both Mme Duthuit and Mr. Schniewind have generously allowed the author to examine their notes.

2. The print reproduced on page 8 has often been called Matisse's first lithograph and has been dated as early as 1904. The year 1907, assigned by Christian Zervos, *Cahiers d'Art,* vol. 6, no. 5–6, 1931, p. 92, seems more likely.

3. In the summer of 1948 Mme Matisse told the author that she herself had cut the three linoleum cuts of 1906. Her husband, she said, drew the designs on the linoleum and then supervised her carving.

4. The lithographs of 1906 are printed on sheets of paper measuring, most frequently, 17¾ x 10¾" (451 x 273 mm). Those of 1914 on sheets 19¾ x 13" (502 x 330 mm).

5. Albert Clinton Landsberg, in a letter to Alfred H. Barr, Jr., quoted in his *Matisse: His Art and His Public,* New York, Museum of Modern Art, 1951, p. 541, note 4.

6. For many years Josette Gris, wife of the painter, has been a close friend of the Matisse family. Gris was often in need of money and Mme Gris posed for Matisse several times. She is characterized in seven of the etchings of 1914.

7. Matisse etched five likenesses of Yvonne Landsberg, perhaps most famous for her painted portrait now owned by the Philadelphia Museum of Art. For the circumstances of the several portraits see Barr, *op. cit.,* pp. 184–5.

8. An etching of the Pont St. Michel has sometimes been assigned to 1914. It was published however by Emile-Paul Frères, *Tableaux de Paris,* Paris, 1927.

9. Walter Pach, *Queer Thing, Painting,* New York, Harper & Brothers, 1938, pp. 219–20.

10. The Matisse-Stravinsky ballet *Le Chant du Rossignol,* first produced by Diaghilev's Ballets Russes in 1920, had been revived, with new choreography, in the spring of 1926.

11. *Dix Danseuses,* an album of 10 lithographs, published by the Editions de la Galerie d'Art Contemporain, Paris, 1927.

12. Mr. Barr's monograph, *op. cit.,* is and probably will remain the authoritative discussion of Matisse's life and work. It contains much information concerning the painter as a printmaker and has been freely consulted here.

13. At the time of his death, he had issued volumes with illustrations by Bonnard, Rodin, Séguin, Bernard, Denis, van Gogh, Dufy, Picasso, Degas, Rouault. He had also contracted, although not published, illustrations by Redon, Roussel, Vuillard, Maillol, Derain, Braque, Segonzac and Chagall.

14. The exhibition took place in Vollard's crowded gallery in the rue Lafitte, June 1–18, 1904.

15. The Vollard album of nudes, never published, was initiated about 1927. It was to have included prints by Bonnard, Chagall, Dufy, Forain, Maillol, Matisse, Picasso, Rouault and others. Editions of these prints were pulled during Vollard's lifetime and have since been individually distributed. Matisse's contribution was an etching, 7¹³⁄₁₆ x 11¹¹⁄₁₆" (198 x 297 mm): a reclining odalisque in pantaloons; she wears a necklace and her hands are folded behind her head.

16. Matisse had presented prints or drawings to four books before 1932. These are in no sense illustrations, but contributions to volumes compiled by friends. Barr, *op. cit.,* pp. 559–60.

17. Other picture dealers had followed the example of Vollard. Daniel Henry Kahnweiler, for instance, issued volumes illustrated by the painters Derain, Picasso, Vlaminck, Braque, Léger, and Gris. Dufy's woodcuts to Apollinaire's *Le Bestiaire* appeared as early as 1911; Maillol's woodblocks to Virgil in 1926.

18. Quotations from the artist are taken from: 1) "Montherlant vu par Matisse," *Beaux-Arts,* August 27th, 1937; 2) Henri Matisse, "Comment je fais mes livres," *Anthologie du livre illustré* edited by Albert Skira, 1944; 3) Henri Matisse, *Jazz,* Paris, Editions Verve, 1947; 4) Adelyn D. Breeskin, "Swans by Matisse," *Magazine of Art,* October, 1935.

19. "The complete maquette for these illustrations

is now a part of the Cone Collection. Included in the group are over 60 drawings, 52 etchings and 29 cancelled etching plates."—Adelyn D. Breeskin, Director of the Baltimore Museum of Art. Most of the preliminary drawings for the etchings appear on the pages where the text has already been printed.

20. See Barr, *op. cit.,* p. 249.

21. It seems probable that Matisse discussed the construction of *Ulysses* with his literary friends. He was acquainted with many avant-garde writers including, of course, his son-in-law Georges Duthuit.

22. In his statement "Comment je fais mes livres," *op. cit.,* Matisse does not even list *Ulysses* among his illustrated books.

23. A collaboration with Vollard was no longer possible. He had died in 1939. It is possible, however, that Vollard in 1937 had instigated the meetings between Matisse and Montherlant in view to a possible publication.

24. Fabiani, the previous year published *Dessins: Thèmes et Variations,* several series of pencil drawings by Matisse gathered together and reproduced as a de luxe edition.

25. *Pasiphaé* was first produced in Paris at the Théâtre Pigalle on December 6, 1938.

26. In 1918 Matisse had contributed five drawings to Pierre Reverdy's *Les jockeys camouflés et période hors-texte;* in 1912 he drew a portrait of Rouveyre

which was used as a frontispiece in a monograph by Louis Thomas.

27. Tériade, as the publisher of *Verve,* frequently reproduced Matisse's paintings and several issues of the magazine bear covers designed by the artist.

28. Matisse first covered sheets of white paper with thin washes of brilliant colors. Then he cut out figures and forms. These he arranged into designs and the "drawings with scissors," as Matisse called them, were reproduced by *pochoir* (stencil) using the same colors the artist himself had mixed.

29. In his *Vingt ans d'activité,* 1948, Albert Skira has written an account of the publication of *Florilège des amours de Ronsard.*

30. Tériade published the *Poèmes de Charles d'Orléans* in 1950. Priced inexpensively as if to emphasize its popular appeal, twelve hundred and thirty copies were printed—about four times as many as in the usual de luxe edition.

31. Since Matisse preferred to make his illustrations while a book was actually in progress, it is doubly fortunate that he had the best possible technical collaboration. Most of his illustrations were printed in Paris by Roger Lacourière for the etchings, the brothers Mourlot for the lithographs. The knowledge, patience and understanding of these master printers contributed substantially to the success of his best volumes.

NOTES TO THE REPRODUCTIONS

The prints, grouped by media, are listed according to their sequence of reproduction. Numbers preceding titles refer to pages. Numbers in parentheses immediately following the specification of medium refer to those used in the catalog of Matisse's graphic work established by his family and also used by Mr. Carl O. Schniewind.

Dimensions are given in inches and millimeters; height precedes width.

FRONTISPIECE: *Woman with Hand to Nose.* 1945. Linoleum cut, 11 x 7¾ inches (281 x 198 mm). Collection Mrs. Bertha M. Slattery, New York.

ETCHINGS AND DRYPOINTS

PAGE

33 *Self Portrait as an Etcher.* 1903. Etching with drypoint (52), 5⅞ x 7¾ inches (149 x 198 mm). The Metropolitan Museum of Art, New York, Dick Fund.

34 *Sketches: Nudes.* 1903. Drypoint (55), first state, 5¹³⁄₁₆ x 4 inches (149 x 100 mm). The Museum of Modern Art, New York.
Sketches: Nudes and Children's Heads. 1903. Drypoint (55), second state, 5¹³⁄₁₆ x 4 inches (149 x 100 mm). Private Collection, New York.

35 *Nude.* 1903. Drypoint (56 bis), 5⅞ x 3⅞ inches (150 x 98 mm). The Museum of Modern Art, New York.
Studies of a Woman in Street Costume. 1903. Drypoint (56 B), 5¾ x 4 inches (148 x 100 mm). The Museum of Modern Art, New York.

36 *Portrait of Bourgeat.* 1914. Etching (23), 7⅛ x 5¹⁄₁₆ inches (180 x 128 mm). The Museum of Modern Art, New York, acquired through the Lillie P. Bliss Bequest.

37 *Portrait of Iturrino.* 1914. Etching (8), 7¹⁵⁄₁₆ x 4⅜ inches (202 x 112 mm). The Metropolitan Museum of Art, New York, Dick Fund.
Joan Massia. 1914. Etching (9), 9⅝ x 7⅝ inches (246 x 194 mm). The Museum of Modern Art, New York, gift of Eugene Victor Thaw.

38 *Yvonne Landsberg.* 1914. Etching (17), 6¼ x 2⅜ inches (159 x 60 mm). The Metropolitan Museum of Art, New York, Dick Fund.
Yvonne Landsberg. 1914. Etching (16), 7⅞ x 4⅜ inches (200 x 110 mm). The Museum of Modern Art, New York, gift of Mr. and Mrs. E. Powis Jones.

39 *Loulou.* 1914. Etching (59 A), 6⁵⁄₁₆ x 2⅜ inches (160 x 61 mm). The Baltimore Museum of Art, Cone Collection.
Loulou. 1914. Etching (58), 6¼ x 2⅜ inches (160 x 60 mm). Private Collection, New York.

40 *Matthew Stewart Prichard.* 1914. Etching (38, second plate), 7⅛ x 4¹³⁄₁₆ inches (182 x 122 mm). The Museum of Modern Art, New York.

41 *Matthew Stewart Prichard.* August, 1914. Etching (38, first plate), 7¹³⁄₁₆ x 5¹³⁄₁₆ (199 x 148 mm). The Museum of Modern Art, New York.

42 *Demetrius Galanis.* 1914. Etching (35), 3½ x 2½ inches (90 x 65 mm). The Museum of Modern Art, New York.
Emma La Forge. 1914. Etching (21), 6¹⁵⁄₁₆ x 4¹⁵⁄₁₆ inches (176 x 126 mm). The Metropolitan Museum of Art, New York, Dick Fund.

43 *Irène Vignier.* 1914. Etching (7), 3½ x 2½ inches (90 x 65 mm). The Metropolitan Museum of Art, New York, Dick Fund.
Irène Vignier. 1914. Etching (2), 7 x 4¾ inches (178 x 120 mm). The Metropolitan Museum of Art, New York, Dick Fund.

44 *Josette Gris.* 1914. Etching (27), 6⁵⁄₁₆ x 2⅜ inches (160 x 60 mm). The Metropolitan Museum of Art, New York, Dick Fund.
Josette Gris. 1914. Etching (26), 6⅛ x 2⅜ inches (157 x 60 mm). The Museum of Modern Art, New York, gift of Mrs. John D. Rockefeller, Jr.

45 *Double Portrait of Josette Gris.* 1914. Etching (32), 5¹⁄₁₆ x 7¹⁄₁₆ inches (129 x 179 mm). The Museum of Modern Art, New York, Mrs. John D. Rockefeller, Jr. Purchase Fund.

46 *Mme Demetrius Galanis.* 1914. Etching (18), 6³⁄₁₆ x 2⅜ inches (160 x 61 mm). The Museum of Modern Art, New York, the Lillie P. Bliss Collection.
Mme Demetrius Galanis. 1914. Etching (20), 6¼ x 2⅜ inches (160 x 60 mm). The Metropolitan Museum of Art, New York, Dick Fund.

47 *Olivares.* 1914. Etching (34), 6¼ x 2⅜ inches (158 x 60 mm). The Metropolitan Museum of Art, New York, Dick Fund.
Walter Pach. 1914. Etching (33), 6⅜ x 2⅜ inches (161 x 61 mm). The Museum of Modern Art, New York.

48 *Woman in a Kimono (Mme Matisse).* 1914. Etching (13), 6⁵⁄₁₆ x 2⅜ inches (160 x 60 mm). The Museum of Modern Art, New York, Mrs. John D. Rockefeller, Jr. Purchase Fund.

49 *The Persian.* 1914. Etching (12), 6⁵⁄₁₆ x 2⅜ inches (160 x 60 mm). The Metropolitan Museum of Art, New York, Dick Fund.
Margot. 1914. Etching (15), 5⅝ x 4 inches (143 x 103 mm). The Metropolitan Museum of Art, New York, Dick Fund.

50 *Marguerite.* 1919. Drypoint (103), 7⅛ x 5⅛ inches (180 x 130 mm). The Museum of Modern Art, New York.
Marguerite (eyes closed). 1919. Etching (108), 5¹⁵⁄₁₆ x 3¹⁵⁄₁₆ inches (151 x 100 mm). The Museum of Modern Art, New York.

51 *Margot in a Japanese Robe.* 1914. Etching (43), 7¹¹⁄₁₆ x 4¼ inches (196 x 107 mm). The Museum of Modern Art, New York, Mrs. John D. Rockefeller, Jr. Purchase Fund.

52 *Reclining Nude with a Goldfish Bowl.* 1929. Etching (155), 6⅝ x 9⅜ inches (168 x 238 mm). The Museum of Modern Art, New York, gift of Mr. and Mrs. E. Powis Jones.

53 *Seated Nude with a Goldfish Bowl.* 1929. Etching (183), 8½ x 6 inches (217 x 153 mm). Collection Mrs. Gertrud A. Mellon, Greenwich, Connecticut.

54 *Seated Nude with a Parrot Cage.* 1929. Etching (180), 6⅞ x 9⅜ inches (175 x 239 mm). The Baltimore Museum of Art, Cone Collection.

55 *Seated Nude with Pictures.* 1929. Etching (95), 8 x 6 inches (204 x 153 mm). The Baltimore Museum of Art, Cone Collection.

56 *Girl before an Aquarium.* 1929. Etching (149), 5 x 7¹⁄₁₆ inches (128 x 179 mm). The Museum of

PAGE

Modern Art, New York.

Girl before an Aquarium. 1929. Etching (156), 3⅝ x 4⅞ inches (92 x 124 mm). The Museum of Modern Art, New York.

57 *Nude on a Couch.* 1929. Etching (136), 3⅝ x 4 13/16 inches (93 x 123 mm). The Museum of Modern Art, New York.

Woman Reading. 1929. Etching (147), 4¼ x 5 13/16 inches (108 x 148 mm). The Museum of Modern Art, New York.

58 *Nude Reclining on a Chaise Longue.* 1929. Etching (64), 5 x 7 inches (127 x 177 mm). Private Collection, New York.

59 *Woman in a Peignoir.* 1929. Etching (86), 10 x 6 inches (255 x 152 mm). Collection Mrs. Gertrud A. Mellon, Greenwich, Connecticut.

60 *Seated Nude (arms crossed).* 1929. Drypoint (117), 5½ x 3 15/16 inches (140 x 100 mm). The Museum of Modern Art, New York.

Seated Nude (*head in arms*). 1929. Etching (176), 7 15/16 x 4¾ inches (201 x 120 mm). Collection Peter H. Deitsch, New York.

61 *Head in Arms.* 1929. Etching (87), 4 x 5¾ inches (101 x 146 mm). Collection Peter H. Deitsch, New York.

LINOLEUM CUTS

65 *Seated Nude.* 1906. Linoleum cut (1), 12¼ x 8 7/16 inches (312 x 215 mm). The Museum of Modern Art, New York, Mrs. John D. Rockefeller, Jr. Purchase Fund.

66 *Seated Nude.* 1906. Linoleum cut (2), 18¾ x 15 inches (475 x 381 mm). The Museum of Modern Art, New York, gift of Mr. and Mrs. R. Kirk Askew, Jr.

67 *Seated Nude.* 1906. Linoleum cut (3), 13½ x 10⅝ inches (342 x 269 mm). The Museum of Modern Art, New York, Mrs. John D. Rockefeller, Jr. Purchase Fund.

MONOTYPES

71 *Seated Nude.* 1914. Monotype, 6¼ x 2⅜ inches (159 x 61 mm). Private Collection, Philadelphia.

72 *Apples on a Plate.* 1914. Monotype, 2¼ x 6⅛ inches (57 x 155 mm). The Museum of Modern Art, New York, Mrs. John D. Rockefeller, Jr. Purchase Fund.

Apples on a Plate. 1914. Monotype, 2⅛ x 6 inches (54 x 153 mm). Collection Mr. and Mrs. E. Powis Jones, New York.

73 *Three Apples.* 1914. Monotype, 3⅝ x 5⅝ inches (92 x 143 mm). Collection E. Weyhe, New York.

74 *Head of a Girl.* 1914. Monotype, 6 x 2¼ inches (153 x 57 mm). Collection Louis Macmillan, New York.

Yvonne Landsberg. 1915. Monotype, 6 3/16 x 2⅜ inches (157 x 60 mm). Collection Walter Pach, New York. Inscribed: "à Walter Pach cordialement Henri-Matisse monotype 1915."

75 *Mme André Derain.* 1914. Monotype, 2½ x 3½ inches (64 x 89 mm). Collection Robert Thomsen, New York.

Irène Vignier. 1914. Monotype, 6⅛ x 2¼ inches (155 x 57 mm). Collection E. Weyhe, New York.

76 *Seated Nude with Arms Crossed*. 1914. Monotype, 7 x 5 inches (177 x 127 mm). The Metropolitan Museum of Art, New York, gift of Stephen Bourgeois.

77 *Torso*. 1914. Monotype, 6¹⁵⁄₁₆ x 5¹⁄₁₆ inches (176 x 128 mm). The Museum of Modern Art, New York, Frank Crowninshield Fund.

78 *Interior: Artist Drawing Three Apples*. 1914. Monotype, 3¹³⁄₁₆ x 5¾ inches (97 x 147 mm). The Museum of Modern Art, New York, Mrs. John D. Rockefeller, Jr. Purchase Fund.

79 *Interior: Artist Drawing Three Apples and Sculpture*. 1914. Monotype, 7¹⁄₁₆ x 5 inches (179 x 128 mm). Collection E. Weyhe, New York.
Still Life with Gourds. 1914. Monotype, 5¹⁄₁₆ x 7¹⁄₁₆ inches (129 x 180 mm). Collection E. Weyhe, New York.

LITHOGRAPHS

83 *Self Portrait*. 1949. Lithograph, 9 x 7¼ inches (230 x 183 mm). The Museum of Modern Art, New York, the Curt Valentin Bequest.

84 *Harbor at Collioure*. 1906. Lithograph (1 bis), 4⁵⁄₁₆ x 7⅝ inches (109 x 194 mm). The Museum of Modern Art, New York, gift in memory of Leo and Nina Stein. Inscribed: "Hommage à Mademoiselle Stein Henri-Matisse."

85 *Head with Eyes Closed*. 1906. Lithograph (1 or 12), 17⁵⁄₁₆ x 10¹³⁄₁₆ inches (440 x 275 mm). The Museum of Modern Art, New York, Mrs. John D. Rockefeller, Jr. Purchase Fund.

86 *Crouching Nude with Black Hair*. 1906. Lithograph (5 bis), 16⅝ x 8¾ inches (422 x 223 mm). The Museum of Modern Art, New York, Larry L. Aldrich Fund.

87 *Crouching Nude with Hands Crossed*. 1906. Lithograph (3), 15½ x 9⅛ inches (392 x 232 mm). Private Collection, New York.

88 *Standing Nude with Downcast Eyes*. 1906. Lithograph (2 bis), 17⅝ x 9½ inches (448 x 242 mm). The Museum of Modern Art, New York, gift in memory of Leo and Nina Stein.

89 *Standing Nude with Arms Folded*. 1906. Lithograph (2 or 6), 17 x 9¹¹⁄₁₆ inches (432 x 245 mm). The Museum of Modern Art, New York, gift of Victor S. Riesenfeld.

90 *Nude Seated in a Folding Chair*. 1906. Lithograph (4), 14¾ x 10⅝ inches (374 x 269 mm). The Museum of Modern Art, New York, gift in memory of Leo and Nina Stein.

91 *Nude with a Foot Stool*. 1906. Lithograph (9), 16⅜ x 7⅝ inches (416 x 193 mm). The Museum of Modern Art, New York, Mrs. John D. Rockefeller, Jr. Purchase Fund.

92 *Nude Seated in a Wicker Chair*. 1914. Lithograph (17), 19 x 11 inches (481 x 279 mm). The Museum of Modern Art, New York, gift of Mrs. John D. Rockefeller, Jr.

93 *Nude*. 1906. Lithograph (11), 17¹⁄₁₆ x 10⅛ inches (434 x 257 mm). The Museum of Modern Art, New York, gift of Mrs. John D. Rockefeller, Jr.

94 *Nude with Face Half Hidden*. 1914. Lithograph (15), 19¾ x 12 inches (503 x 305 mm). The Museum of Modern Art, New York, Frank Crowninshield Fund.

95 *Back*. 1914. Lithograph (19), 16⅝ x 10⅜ inches (421 x 264 mm). The Metropolitan Museum of Art, New York, Rogers Fund.

96 *Upturned Head*. 1906. Lithograph (5), 11⅛ x 10¾ inches (283 x 274 mm). The Museum of Modern Art, New York, gift of Mrs. John D. Rockefeller, Jr.

97 *Black Eyes.* 1914. Lithograph (18), 17⅞ x 12¾ inches (453 x 326 mm). The Museum of Modern Art, New York, gift of Mrs. Saidie A. May.

98 *Seated Girl in Garden.* 1922. Lithograph (36), 16⅛ x 20⅜ inches (410 x 518 mm). The Baltimore Museum of Art, Cone Collection.

99 *Girl Reading.* 1925. Lithograph (78), 6¼ x 9⅝ inches (160 x 246 mm). The Baltimore Museum of Art, Cone Collection.

100 *The Organdy Dress.* 1922. Lithograph (38), 16¾ x 10¹³⁄₁₆ inches (426 x 275 mm). The Museum of Modern Art, New York, gift of Mrs. John D. Rockefeller, Jr.

101 *Odalisque with a Samovar.* 1929. Lithograph (122), 11⅛ x 14⅞ inches (282 x 377 mm). Collection Peter H. Deitsch, New York.

102 *Girl with a Vase of Flowers.* 1923. Lithograph (50), 7¹⁄₁₆ x 10⁵⁄₁₆ inches (178 x 260 mm). The Museum of Modern Art, New York, Lillie P. Bliss Collection.

103 *Girl with a Vase of Flowers.* 1923. Lithograph (51), 10⅞ x 7½ inches (276 x 191 mm). The Museum of Modern Art, New York, gift of Mrs. John D. Rockefeller, Jr.

104 *The Arab Blouse.* 1925. Lithograph (70), 21¼ x 17⅛ inches (541 x 436 mm). The Museum of Modern Art, New York, Mrs. John D. Rockefeller, Jr. Purchase Fund.

105 *Alfred Cortot.* 1926. Lithograph (82), 15 x 15⅛ inches (381 x 385 mm). The Museum of Modern Art, New York, acquired through the Lillie P. Bliss Bequest.
Study of Legs. 1925. Lithograph (71), 9¾ x 19¾ inches (249 x 504 mm). The Museum of Modern Art, New York, Larry L. Aldrich Fund.

106 *Arabesque.* 1924. Lithograph (58), 19¹⁄₁₆ x 12⅝ inches (485 x 322 mm). The Museum of Modern Art, New York, Lillie P. Bliss Collection.

107 *Reclining Nude.* 1926. Lithograph (84), 17⅜ x 21⅜ inches (442 x 543 mm). M. Knoedler & Co., New York.

108 *Seated Nude with Arms Raised.* 1924. Lithograph (55), 24¼ x 18¹³⁄₁₆ inches (617 x 478 mm). The Museum of Modern Art, New York, Mrs. John D. Rockefeller, Jr. Purchase Fund.

109 *Seated Nude with Arms Raised.* 1925. Lithograph (63), 25⅛ x 18⅞ inches (638 x 480 mm). The Museum of Modern Art, New York, Mrs. John D. Rockefeller, Jr. Purchase Fund.

110 *Odalisque in Striped Pantaloons.* 1925. Lithograph (64), 21½ x 17⅜ inches (546 x 442 mm). Collection Nelson A. Rockefeller, New York.

111 *Odalisque in a Tulle Skirt.* 1928. Lithograph (107), 11 x 14¾ inches (285 x 377 mm). M. Knoedler & Co., New York.
Seated Odalisque. 1928? Lithograph (106), 11¼ x 14 inches (286 x 355 mm). Collection Peter H. Deitsch, New York.

112 *Reclining Dancer.* 1927. Lithograph (96), 9⅞ x 16¼ inches (252 x 414 mm). The Museum of Modern Art, New York, gift of Mrs. Saidie A. May.

113 *Standing Dancer.* 1927. Lithograph (99), 18⅛ x 11 inches (460 x 277 mm). The Museum of Modern Art, New York, gift of Mrs. Saidie A. May.

114 *Reclining Nude with Table.* 1928–29. Lithograph (118), 21⅞ x 18¼ inches (556 x 460 mm). Collection Peter H. Deitsch, New York.

115 *Reclining Nude with Stove.* 1928–29. Lithograph (120), 22 x 18 inches (559 x 462 mm). The Museum of Modern Art, New York, Mrs. John D. Rockefeller, Jr. Purchase Fund.

116 *Reclining Nude.* 1929. Lithograph (121), 18⅛ x 22 inches (460 x 560 mm). Collection Peter H. Deitsch, New York.

141 Etching illustrating the poem *Apparition,* page 15 of *Poésies de Stéphane Mallarmé,* 1932. Page size 13 x 9¾ inches (330 x 247 mm). The Museum of Modern Art, New York, Mrs. John D. Rockefeller, Jr. Purchase Fund.

142 *The Blinding of Polyphemus.* Soft ground etching illustrating *Ulysses* by James Joyce, 1935. Page size 11⅝ x 8⅞ inches (295 x 226 mm). The Museum of Modern Art, New York.

143 *The Caves of the Winds.* Soft ground etching illustrating *Ulysses* by James Joyce, 1935. Page size 11⅝ x 8⅞ inches (295 x 226 mm). The Museum of Modern Art, New York.

144 Linoleum cut frontispiece and title page of *Pasiphaé—Chant de Minos (Les Crétois)* by Henry de Montherlant, 1937–44. Page size 12⅞ x 9¾ inches (328 x 247 mm). The Museum of Modern Art, New York.

Partial text, linoleum cut initial and illustration to the line . . . *seule, au pied du grand caroubier* . . . pages 70–71 of *Pasiphaé—Chant de Minos (Les Crétois)* by Henry de Montherlant, 1937. –44. Page size 12⅞ x 9¾ inches (328 x 247 mm). The Museum of Modern Art, New York.

145 Linoleum cut illustrating the line . . . *Et il faudra mourir sans avoir tué le vent* . . . , page 23 of *Pasiphaé—Chant de Minos (Les Crétois)* by Henry de Montherlant, 1937?–44. Page size 12⅞ x 9¾ inches (328 x 247 mm). The Museum of Modern Art, New York.

146 Color lithograph frontispiece and title page of *Poèmes de Charles d'Orléans,* 1943–50. Page size 16⅛ x 10½ inches (410 x 267 mm). The Museum of Modern Art, New York, Mrs. John D. Rockefeller, Jr. Purchase Fund.

Color lithograph and text of the rondeau beginning *Il me pleust bien* . . . , pages 10–11 of *Poèmes de Charles d'Orléans,* 1943–50. Page size 16⅛ x 10½ inches (410 x 267 mm). The Museum of Modern Art, New York, Mrs. John D. Rockefeller, Jr. Purchase Fund.

147 Color lithograph and text of the ballad beginning *Belle, bonne, nonpareille, plaisant* . . . , pages 22–23 of *Poèmes de Charles d'Orléans,* 1943–50. Page size 16⅛ x 10½ inches (410 x 267 mm). The Museum of Modern Art, New York, Mrs. John D. Rockefeller, Jr. Purchase Fund.

Color lithograph illustrating pages 48–49 of *Poèmes de Charles d'Orléans,* 1943–50. Page size 16⅛ x 10½ inches (410 x 267 mm). The Museum of Modern Art, New York, Mrs. John D. Rockefeller, Jr. Purchase Fund.

148 Lithograph frontispiece and title page of *Florilège des Amours de Ronsard,* 1941–48. Page size 15 x 11 inches (382 x 280 mm). The Museum of Modern Art, New York.

Text and lithograph illustrating the poem beginning *Petit nombril, que mon penser adore* . . . , pages 26–27 of *Florilège des Amours de Ronsard,* 1941–48. Page size 15 x 11 inches (382 x 280 mm). The Museum of Modern Art, New York.

149 Lithograph and partial text of the poem *Elégie à Janet,* pages 42–43 of *Florilège des Amours de Ronsard,* 1941–48. Page size 15 x 11 inches (382 x 280 mm).

Lithograph illustrating the poem beginning *Sous le crystal d'une argenteuse rive* . . . , pages 14–15 of *Florilège des Amours de Ronsard,* 1941–48. Page size 15 x 11 inches (382 x 280 mm). The Museum of Modern Art, New York.

150 Photo-lithograph and partial text of the poem *Sed non satiata,* pages 52–53 of *Les fleurs du mal* by Charles Baudelaire, 1947. Page size 11 x 9 inches (280 x 229 mm). The Museum of Modern Art, New York.

Lithograph illustrating *Les Lettres portugaises* by Marianna Alcaforado, 1946. Page size 10⅝ x 8¼ inches (270 x 210 mm). Collection Pierre Matisse, New York.

BOOKS ILLUSTRATED BY MATISSE

Poésies de Stéphane Mallarmé. Lausanne, Albert Skira et Cie., 1932. 29 etchings. Limited to 145 copies

James Joyce, *Ulysses.* New York, The Limited Editions Club, 1935. Volume designed by George Macy. 6 etchings, each accompanied by 2–5 reproductions of preliminary drawings. Limited to 1500 copies

Henry de Montherlant, *Pasiphaé—Chant de Minos (Les Crétois).* Paris, Martin Fabiani, 1944. 18 full page linoleum cuts; also cover, linoleum-cut ornaments and initials. Limited to 250 copies

Pierre Reverdy, *Visages.* Paris, Editions du Chêne, 1946. 14 full page lithographs; also cover, linoleum-cut ornaments and initials. Limited to 250 copies

André Rouveyre, *Repli.* Paris, Editions du Bélier, 1947. Volume designed by Matisse. 12 full page lithographs; also cover, linoleum-cut ornaments and initials. Limited to 370 copies

Marianna Alcaforado, *Les Lettres portugaises.* Paris, Tériade, 1946. Volume designed by Matisse. 19 full page lithographs; also cover, lithograph ornaments and initials. Limited to 270 copies

Charles Baudelaire, *Les Fleurs du mal.* Paris, La Bibliothèque Française, 1947. Volume designed by Matisse. 1 etching, 33 photo-lithographs, 69 wood engravings reproducing drawings; also cover, ornaments and initials. Limited to 320 copies

Henri Matisse, *Jazz.* Paris, Tériade, 1947. Volume designed by Matisse. 152 pages of text and color stencils. Full and double page color stencil illustrations; text reproduces in facsimile the artist's handwriting; also cover. Limited to 270 copies. Also album of the 20 color stencils without text, limited to 100 copies

Florilège des Amours de Ronsard. Paris, Albert Skira, 1948. Volume designed by Matisse. 126 lithographs consisting of full page illustrations and ornaments; also cover. Limited to 320 copies

Poèmes de Charles d'Orléans. Paris, Tériade, 1950. Volume designed by Matisse. 100 pages of text and lithographs. Full page lithograph illustrations, lithograph ornaments for each page of text which reproduces in facsimile the artist's transcript of the poems; also cover. Limited to 1,230 copies

ETCHINGS AND DRYPOINTS

33

34

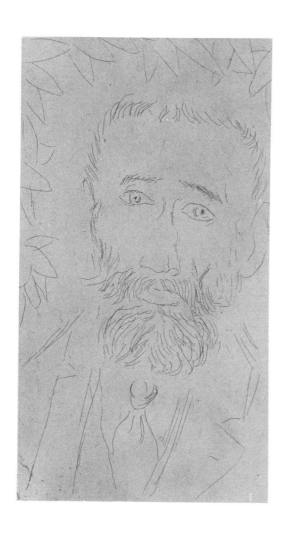

42

46

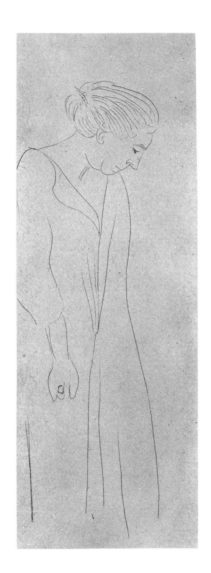

48

56

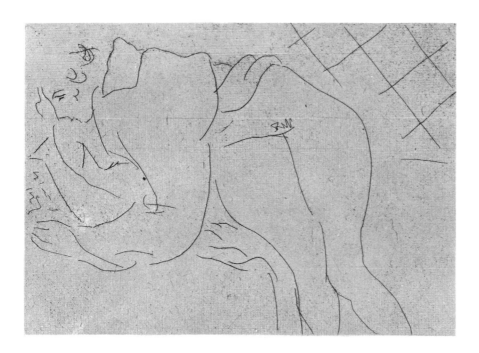

58

LINOLEUM CUTS

MONOTYPES

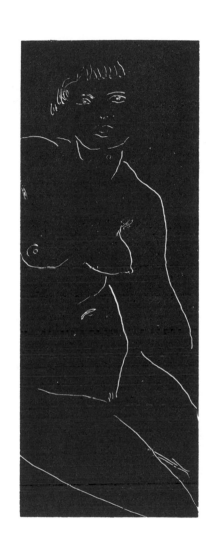

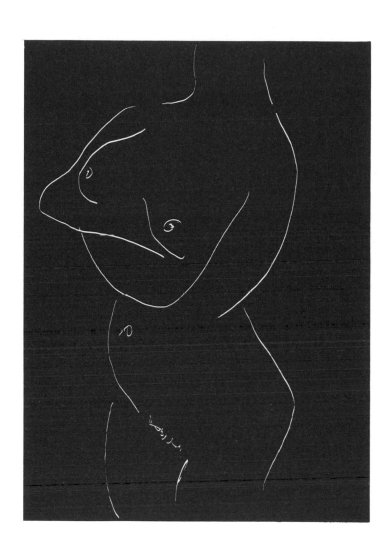

LITHOGRAPHS

HM 15/25

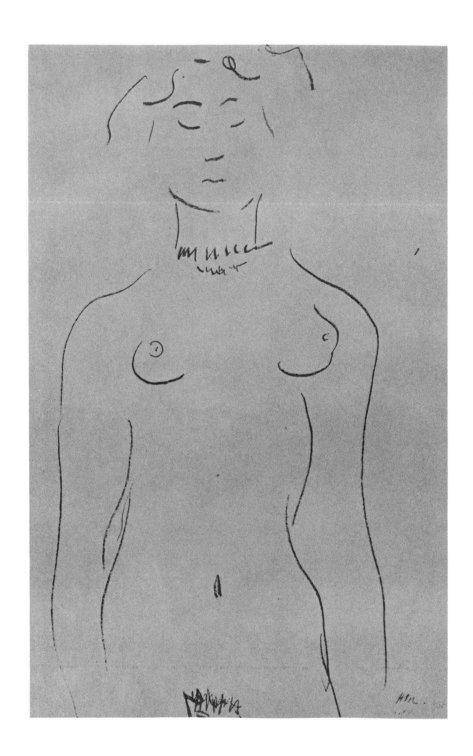

88

90

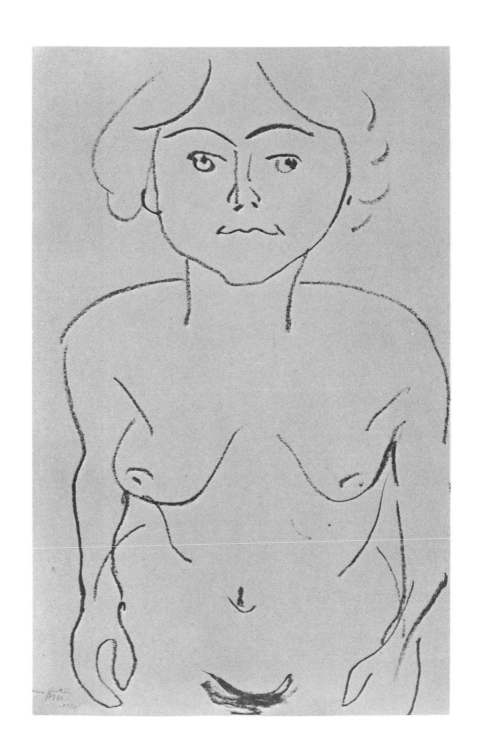

25/504 m

98

103

48/50   Henri Matisse

104

105

108

109

116

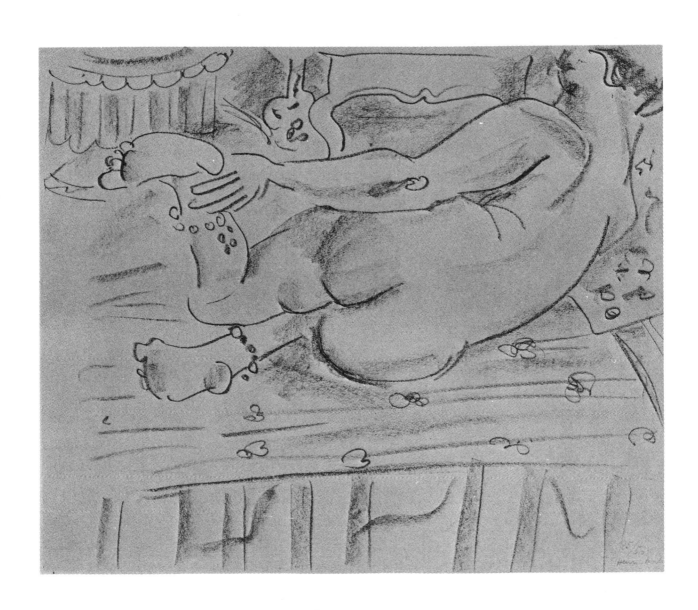

AQUATINTS

ILLUSTRATIONS

131

133

134

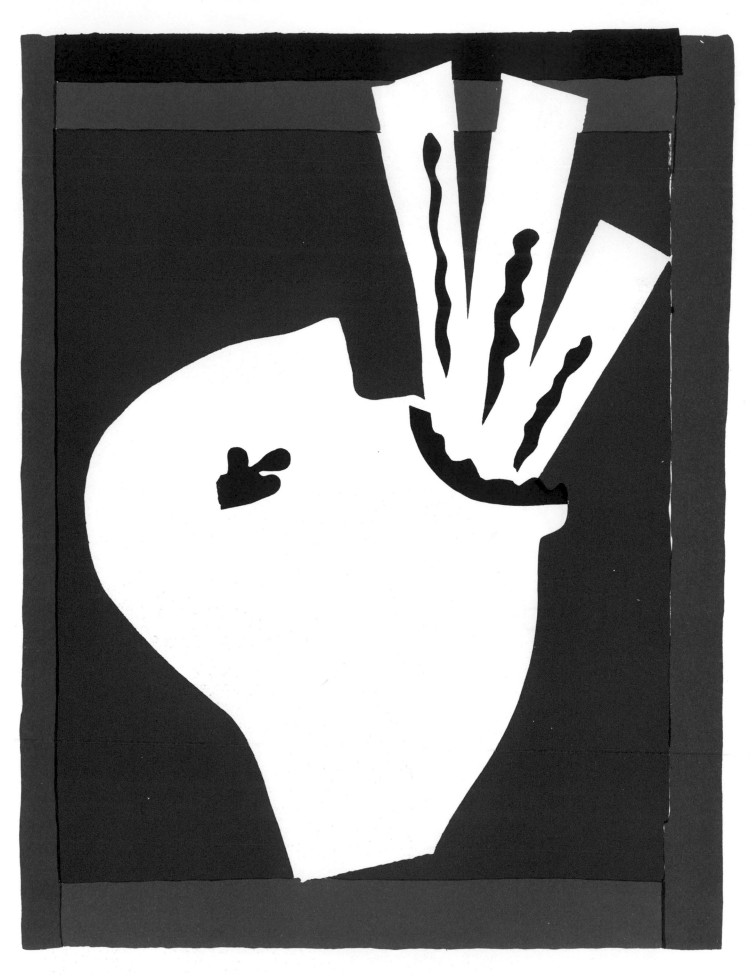

136

Transparente, la fleur qu'il a sentie, enfant,
Au filigrane bleu de l'âme se greffant.
Et, la mort telle avec le seul rêve du sage,
Serein, je vais choisir un jeune paysage
Que je peindrais encor sur les tasses, distrait.
Une ligne d'azur mince & pâle serait
Un lac, parmi le ciel de porcelaine nue,
Un clair croissant perdu par une blanche nue
Trempe sa corne calme en la glace des eaux,
Non loin de trois grands cils d'émeraude, roseaux.

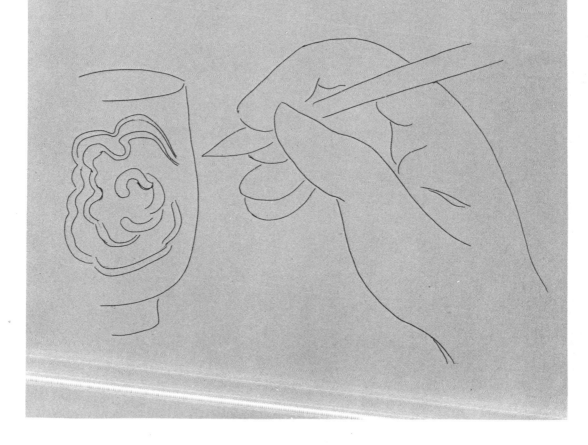

Ses purs ongles très haut dédiant leur onyx,
L'Angoisse, ce minuit, soutient, lampadophore,
Maint rêve vespéral brûlé par le Phénix
Que ne recueille pas de cinéraire amphore

Sur les crédences, au salon vide : nul ptyx,
Aboli bibelot d'inanité sonore
(Car le Maître est allé puiser des pleurs au Styx
Avec ce seul objet dont le Néant s'honore).

Mais proche la croisée au nord vacante, un or
Agonise selon peut-être le décor
Des licornes ruant du feu contre une nixe,

Elle, défunte nue en le miroir, encor
Que, dans l'oubli fermé par le cadre, se fixe
De scintillations sitôt le septuor.

128

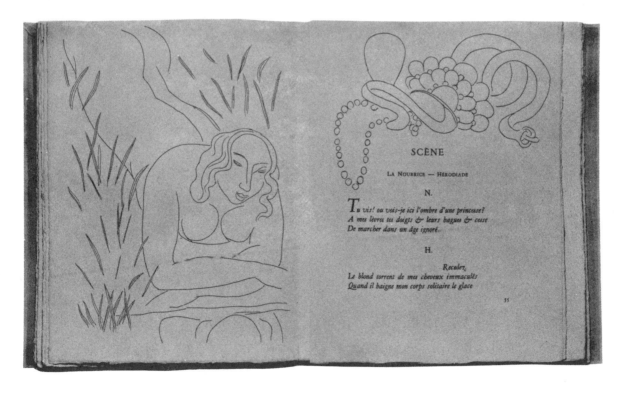

SCÈNE

La Nourrice — Hérodiade

N.

Tu vis! ou vois-je ici l'ombre d'une princesse?
A mes lèvres tes doigts & leurs bagues & cesse
De marcher dans un âge ignoré.

H.

Reculez.
Le blond torrent de mes cheveux immaculés
Quand il baigne mon corps solitaire le glace

55

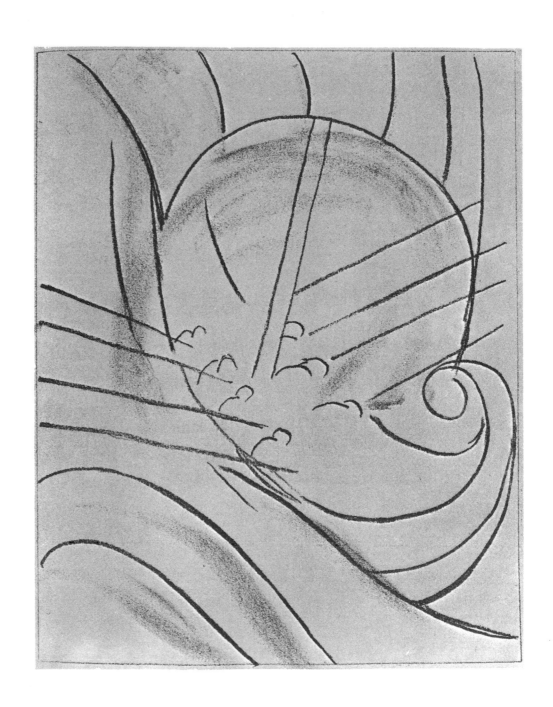

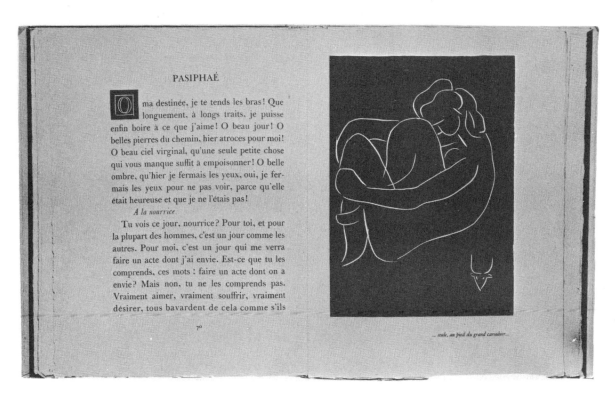

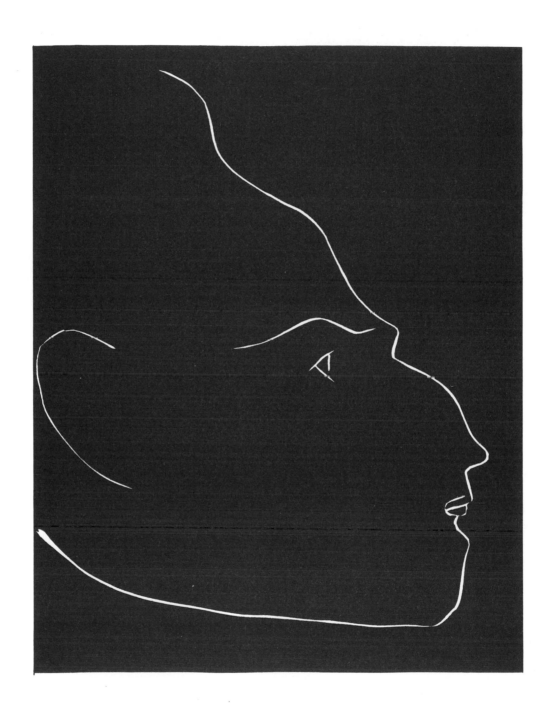

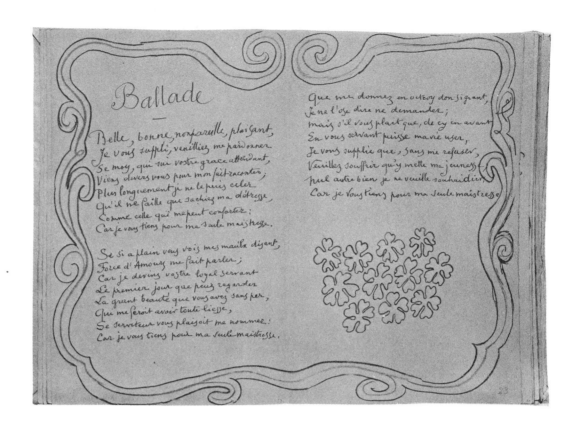

147

FLORILÈGE
DES AMOURS
DE
RONSARD
PAR
HENRI MATISSE

ALBERT SKIRA PARIS

PETIT nombril, que mon penser adore,
Et non mon œil, qui n'eut onques le bien
Que de te voir, et qui mérites bien
Que quelque ville on te bastisse encore.

Signe amoureux, duquel Amour s'honore,
Representant l'Androgyne lien,
Et le courroux du grand Saturnien,
Dont le nombril tousjours se rememore.

N'y ce beau chef, ny ces yeux, ny ce front,
Ny ce beau sein où les fleches se font,
Que les beautez diversement se forgent,

26

Ne me pourroient la douleur alenter,
Sans esperer quelque jour de taster
Ton compagnon, où les amours se logent.

Pein son menton au milieu fosselu,
Et que le bout en rondeur pommelu
Soit tout ainsi que l'on voit apparoistre
Le bout d'un coin qui ja commence à croistre.

Plus blanc que laict caillé dessus le jonc
Pein luy le col, mais pein-le un petit long,
Gresle et charnu : et sa gorge douillette
Comme le col soit un petit longuette.

Apres fay luy par un juste compas,
Et de Junon les coudes et les bras,
Et les beaux doigts de Minerve, et encore
La main egale à celle de l'Aurore.

Je ne sçay plus, mon Janet, où j'en suis :
Je suis confus, et muet : je ne puis
Comme j'ay fait, te declarer le reste

42

izarre déité, brune comme les nuits,
Au parfum mélangé de musc et de havane,
Œuvre de quelque obi, le Faust de la savane,
Sorcière au flanc d'ébène, enfant des noirs minuits,

Je préfère au constance, à l'opium, aux nuits,
L'élixir de ta bouche où l'amour se pavane;
Quand vers toi mes désirs partent en caravane,
Tes yeux sont la citerne où boivent mes ennuis.

Par ces deux grands yeux noirs, soupiraux de ton âme,
O démon sans pitié! verse-moi moins de flamme;
Je ne suis pas le Styx pour t'embrasser neuf fois,

53

de vostre cœur, et de vostre fortune; sur tout, venez me voir.

DIEU, je ne puis quitter ce papier, il tombera entre vos mains, je voudrois bien avoir le mesme bonheur: Hélas! insensée que je suis, je m'apperçois bien que cela n'est pas possible. Adieu, je n'en puis plus. Adieu, aymez-moy toujours; et faites-moy souffrir encore plus de maux.

Seconde Lettre